Dancing

with

Shadow

and

Light

Dancing
with
Shadow
and
Light

poetry by
Jacqueline Miller

Published by Light Dancing Press

ISBN: 979-8-9911576-0-5

Printed in the United States of America

Cover design and typography by David Sand
Heart photo by Donna Hollinshead
Photos of Jacqueline Miller by Andrea Presberg
Cover photo and all other photos by Jacqueline Miller

Visit the author at
www.dancingwithshadowandlight.com
Write the author at
jackie@dancingwithshadowandlight.com

For Andrea
my constant support and beloved companion through life

Table of Contents

Light

Acknowledgments

Biography

Introduction

This book is a journey of healing through the spiritual heart. I hope this book will move you and stimulate your imagination. You will find tools for moving from shadow to light, depression to hope, and judgment to acceptance. It is a guide for the way out and through, and speaks of our common human struggles and the power of the heart. It is a story of the beauty of nature, love and Spirit.

Beloved is one of the words I use for the divine source. Use whatever word works for you—God, goddess, the universe, creation, the One.

Have fun. Experience the world from different angles. Allow your imagination to take flight. I hope you find enjoyment, fresh perspectives, healing and upliftment through your own dance with shadow and Light.

—Jackie

Healing

In peace and joy, I celebrate all pieces of myself

Merry Go Round

Round and round it turns
filled with great beasts and horses
ridden without fear
in their familiarity

Round and round
in comfortable repetition
nothing expected but to ride
up and down in mechanical rhythm

As I turn the corner
a pretty brass ring appears
always a bit out of reach
though I stand in the stirrups
stretching for the prize

Round and round
half tranced in monotony
the circular motion safe and secure
knowing what each moment will bring

When I get off the beast
and move to the edge
I get dizzy and afraid to leave
the zone of comfort I've constructed

Can I jump and be safe?

In a leap of faith I jump
and am out and about
exploring the worlds
both inner and outer

Then I am back again
riding the beasts in circular motion
round and round I turn
exhausted by the sameness
of the all too familiar pattern of my life

I know surrender is the answer
so I might transcend
to the next level
of my growth in Spirit

To create spirals rather than
circles that lead nowhere
and explore the many worlds
existing in the now

I give up and let go
into the blessed fullness
of the present moment
teeming with the Divine

Empathetic Heart

The heart
spirit's guide
site of joy and loving
trembles
as waves of despair and loss bombard

The heart
builds panels to protect
with gaps between so emotions seep in
an illusion of protection

When the gate opens
the rawness of the projected emotions enter
ripping the heart into ragged pieces
creating an opportunity in the fields of destruction
for a new formation

A gift of transmutation
in the sharing of empathetic pain
an emergence of love
freed from the scattered walls of illusion

Love pouring forth
in shared communion
carrying forth golden light
and the healing rays of an overflowing heart

Ode to the Ego

My ego wears a clown suit
juggling balls of distraction

My ego, dressed in a straw boater hat and cane
dances and sings in a vaudeville act

My ego plays so wise
dressing in a monk's robe to lead me astray

My ego is a navigator
steering me off course

My ego builds a fortress
keeping all at bay

My ego is a tyrant
intent upon control

My ego is an illusionist
creating false realities

My ego is a judge
meting out punishment in laws it writes itself

My ego is a quick change artist
changing outfits and roles

My ego is a jester
laughing as a fool

My ego is a savior
lost in a dream of good

My ego is a protector
thinking that it rules

My ego is a servant
providing for my needs

When tamed, I find my ego
a very useful friend

The Shadow

The sun is high with a bright light
I search the ground below
I see a shape that lives in me
a shadow huge and grim

I move my hands and make a claw
to model how it feels
A hulky shape that takes control
to turn my life askew

Its claws grab me when I take flight
to hold me on the ground
And when I fly it holds me tight
to keep me in its sight

I twist and turn so I can leave
to find the hidden doors
To search within and search without
for the secret key
that turns the lock releasing me
to be the all of me

And so we clash
in push and pull
in some enchanted lock
Until I stop and turn around
to face the monster feared

I say hello, what do you want?
How can I help you heal?

Gently reaching out my hand
I bring the shadow close
holding it in warm embrace
I say in gentle voice
I love you as you are my dear
thanks for all you've done

Let us go in harmony and
walk the hidden way
The path lights up with inner love
and frees the wisest self

In peace and joy I celebrate
all pieces of myself

Click

Click ... Click ... Click
I turn my eye like a kaleidoscope
each turn bringing a different picture of reality

Click
I see visions of angels watching over me

Click
I see the pain and hurt of the loyal opposition

Click
The pieces fall into place to form a new universe

Click
The darkness spreads anger and hatred raining
down on the world

Click
The land is filled with abundance

Click
I'm caught in my positions and judgments

Click
My heart opens as love pours forth for all

Click ... click ... click
I make myself dizzy with endless possibilities

Click
I am still and listen, taking in the melodious
sounds of the universe

Click
It all comes into focus, my path is clear

Click
Light and matrixes everywhere

Click
And I am holy here

Paper Wraps Around Rock

Sometimes life seems exhausting
bombarded by bad news
  war
  hatred
  corruption
  mistreatment

An endless litany of complaints and pain

What can I do about it
but change my focus from evil to Light
to stand with the Light bearers
who pray for an end to againstness
and a surrender into peace

How not to judge this upheaval
in the world and in the human heart?
Going for peace is the only end for aggression
giving up the need to win at all costs
in a zero sum game

We cycle over and over again
the same tired patterns
following the whisperers of the dark

So I stand with the silent ones
holding the Light
praying for love to wrap around hate
like in the childhood game
paper wraps around rock and overcomes
Love transmutes hate

Fragments

Fragments
a thought
a dream
a piece of prayer
scattered in the tornado in my head

I chase them
trying to gather the scraps
turning and twisting
changing direction in a whirlwind
hoping to capture it all
and form some cohesive whole

Making myself dizzy in my effort
I grab a chip of my imagination
and stop

A fragment
It is enough to build a truth upon
and feel myself whole

The Birds

My mind lost in thought
searches for meaning

And then I hear the sound of birds
  tweet, tweet, hoot, hoot
and fall in love with the song
marveling at the voices of these
aerodynamic creations of God

I'm back to the unfinished
my burning questions
and hear again
the melody of the birds
calling to each other
allowing me to listen in

Then there is a silence
a siren in the background
the murmur of the trees
I return again to the diversions
of my mind

The birds begin again
lifting me to another reality
where all is simple and in accord
Illusions shred, peace descends
I stop and listen again

Moment

I want... I want...I want
in endless litany
each want a separation
a pushing away of the present moment
and the joy with that which is

I search for answers, for meaning
and leave the moment

I ignore the whispers of the new flower
beginning to peek from the ground
The glistening drops of water
changing with the angle of the light
The passing dragon fly
iridescent as it moves it's wings

I yearn for a more perfect world
for justice and fairness for all
for clear and breathable air
crystalline waters, robust forests
and deny myself the gift of acceptance
in the beauty of the moment

I come to balance
accepting that all can exist at the same time
I center in the present and
fill with the healing and peace
available in each Spirit filled moment

Maze

When I judge and compare
I enter the maze of confusion
Going through the hedges
I look for a way to the center and out
lost to wander in the labyrinth of my mind

Until I pause and center in the moment
releasing the flotsam of the mind's contents
into the ethers
and rest in the knowing of the heart

I send love to the judgments
of right and wrong
of good and evil
that I may heal myself and
the creatures of the earth with love

As I open
my vision clears
and I see the path ahead
leading me to the center of my being
and embrace the Allness of it All

Come to Me

Come to me Beloved
gently enter the essence of my being
fill me and free me to be
bigger and fuller than
this finite ego that seems to rule me

I desire only to drop my bursting head
on your soft shoulder
You gently touch my face and hair
whispering your love to me
I whisper back my adoration
and my passion to be one

Until all difference fades
and my breath becomes your breath
my heart beats to the rhythm of your center
that is All

Slowly as we merge
I hear your names in rolling waves through me
You teach me to open myself
without reservation to you
and that you reside in me at all times

I need only to close my eyes and lean on you
Knowing you enfold me in your
constant warmth and loving
You protect me as I stumble and fall
You rock me as I drift to sleep
and rise to the source of my Soul

Oh God how can I ever forget you
You send messengers to lead me home
when I feel I have lost my way
All that you ask is that I trust
yield to your mystery and
follow the way you have shown

The Oceans

Spirit flowing
water in the oceans of the universe
always available for those who would partake
and open to the infinite flow
awake and present to the ever circulating streams

I know this, yet I feel thirsty
yearning to be filled
in my empty longing for oneness
in my illusion I have turned off the spigot

I bottle up the flow
cutting off my connection
to the source of all things
as I fall down the rabbit hole of hunger and want

Knowing on some level
all I need to do is open the faucet
No, tear out the plumbing of my civilization
and let the water flow unhindered

Freely bathing
God's spirit flowing through me
I move in the never ending river
and set sail on the oceans of the many worlds

Medicine Woman

Medicine woman
Dancing with power
Knowing the truth of connection
to the source
Aware of the threads that join us
to the beating heart that lives in all

Medicine woman
Laughing in union
with the earth and the sky
Seeing the shining threads in
ever changing patterns and colors

Medicine woman
Joyous lover
sharing the truth
of the wisdom of the heart
in healing song and word

Medicine woman
Weaving the webs
found deep in the earth
spanning time and dimension

Wild Woman

I sit as judge and jury
filled with the voices that live in my mind
ready to deliver the verdict
and mete out punishment
to my guilty self

Will it be hard labor in a cell
of my own making
or a sentence to learn the proper behavior
of a woman in the world

To follow laws imposed by some
imaginary belief
that I must be constrained
to control the wildness living inside

Is it time to let the wild woman out to
blaze in the world in all her glory?

Knowing all along that I have the key
and am ready to open the door
to let the outlaw out
the maker of her own rules

To run free spewing rainbows of light
cavorting with my gang of masters
sharing words of wisdom drafted by Spirit
released on the winds to spiral forth
carried by the Light on wings of love
in joyful adventure and endless expansion

Wild woman
dancing and laughing in joy
in oneness with You

On the Edge

I stop on the edge
    waiting
        waiting for the right moment
        waiting
            waiting

Waiting for the wind to move me
    waiting
        waiting for the push
            into the void

I stop on the edge
    waiting
        afraid to take the step into the unknown
          into the unknowable

I stand on the edge
    waiting
        waiting for the wind
            waiting for the thrust that never comes

I stand on the edge
    knowing
        the wind, the push
            must come from inside

I stand on the edge
    waiting
        waiting for the voices
            to tell me it's time

I stand on the edge
    gathering focus
        the strength from within
            knowing the journey is set to begin

I stand on the edge
    waiting
        and notice I've stepped
        and have been flying all along

Through the Desert

I

When I am void of you Beloved
I am in a wasteland
walking a path in the desert
barren and dry
lost in the wilderness as I roam
like the lost tribes
looking for the promised land
the land of your being
I know you are my oasis
on the journey I have embarked upon

I lose direction and look around
  North — nothing but sand
  South — aridness and want lie that way
  East — the sun rises and burns,
    the earth is parched
  West — the distant mountains are barren
    and unwelcoming

No place to go in this desolate landscape
shattered by the drying bones
I have left behind me
Nowhere to go but within
taking an alternate route to You
my salvation, my God

II

I pray to you Beloved
knowing only you can
bring lushness and life to the desert
You are the promised land of milk and honey
I burrow down through the layers of
dry earth and rock
the unfertile ground I have created
I notice a growing moisture
as new life begins to form

Spring begins with subtle growth
above ground
as strong roots are formed below
Digging deeper the lushness grows
a deep well is struck
freeing your Being to pour forth
to water the arid landscape
with your Light and joyous loving

III

The beauty that was always there
begins to flower
Torrents of your bounty pour forth
on the newly awakened land
watering the once deserted territory
enlivening the surface

Suddenly wildflowers fill the horizon
Pools of water appear
igniting the chain of life
A waterfall can be heard in the distance
Forests sprout from nothingness
Green fields and meadows grow
The mountains in the distance become
lush places of beauty
Life in its multitude emerges
from the darkness
Your creatures drink in the
depths of your lakes
eat on the richness of your land
multiply in joyous affirmation of your Being

IV

Looking around in awe at your creation
I know my journey is through
I remember again the promised land
is not some distant unattainable place
but here, now, to be found
each time I turn to You
and I surrender to your power
allowing You to burn away the inessential
so I may enter into
the sweet land of your salvation

Imagine

To love it all and dream it all

Surfing Through Time

I ride the waves of time
timelessly surfing
the infinite ocean of being
Weaving through each moment of balance
as the waves carry me
through calm and turbulent waters
into the present moment

As I surf I travel
I am here committed to the present moment
Time speeds as I travel back to 820..1960..1541
back and back and yet still here
Balancing on my board
through the infinite point of the center
that is the present
I sequence through time

My mind tries to understand
and I lose my balance
about to fall into the endless bottom
I steady myself again and feel the
roughness of the board beneath me
my bare feet prickling
with the texture and support
of the now that is all

Riding through time, wind in my face
past, future, now
unable to sort the difference
I let myself be carried
by the undulating waves

Each precious moment of now
opening endless oceans
of time and space
Who knows where I will be carried next
as I practice being present and
explore the infinite moment

A Study of Shadow and Light

Shadow and light flit across the marsh grass
creating a scene of beauty
Splashes of light against the dark
a luminance that can only be seen
against the shadow

And so it is in the world
light and shadow co-existing
The light illuminates as it pierces and shines
creating a new form
magnificent to behold

A transcendent beauty
connecting all
in shared vibration
to the One

Tightrope Walker

I walk a tightrope
spanning two worlds
the visible and invisible
Voices call from each *come to me and stay*

I walk a tightrope
wobbling this way and that
in my effort for balance
so as not to plunge into the chasm

I walk a tightrope
spanning two worlds
afraid to lose my balance
and lose control

The rope is thin
the edges frayed
yet it holds me in my steps
between the universes

I walk a tightrope
holding strong
as I listen to the voices and
music from beyond

I walk a tightrope
steady as I go
a buttress against the wind
that would knock me off balance if it could

I walk a tightrope
between the worlds
carrying messages back and forth

In a flash, I see the whole
a web of lattices
walkers on all

Souls filled with light
walking the tightropes
weaving a grid that unites us

I walk a tightrope
between the worlds
describing marvels of blessed kin
joined by matrixes woven through time

If I Could

If I could
I would spend my days
with the masters
wandering the halls of time and space
wide-eyed to the wonders
that abound in the universes
head in the air
ignoring the ground that I stand upon

Why return to the humdrum world
of need and pain?
Rather I would fly through dimensions
leaping into the quantum matrix
knowing not where I would land
loving the Spirit in it all

Yet here I am planted on the earth
drinking of the earth mother
feeling the magic and radiance
of her earthly cycles
dazzled by the beauty and abundance
provided yet so often ignored

Planting my feet
reaching into the heavens
I declare my place
a column
anchoring the light from above
drawing from the richness below

As earth and sky are one
so am I
Spirit cycles through me
as above so below
in endless harmony
the rhythm of life and eternity

A Poem Forms

I ask and somehow
a poem appears
bare boned
waiting to be filled

A sight, a sound, a scent
the beginning of a shape
a glimpse into the invisible
stir life

A beat, a drum, singing love
and the heart is formed
to give meaning to it all

A vessel to be filled
with the gift of Spirit
bringing the soul of the poem to fruition
and the rhythm of the poem to life

A Dream of Flying

I float above observing
gliding this way and that
to take in the whole picture

The beauty that radiates below
is illuminated from the light above
creating light and shadow over the land

The drifting air carries me on puffs of wind
my imaginary wings outstretched
to catch each current

I love the sky and what's beyond
it lifts me from the earth
I join the birds and those above
to fly on angels wings

I do a loop
turn on my back
rejoice that I'm alive
to love it all and dream it all

I celebrate and soar

Water

I think of the strength of water
a gentle flow surmounting all obstacles
streaming over rocks and around boulders
over hills into waterfalls
carving rivers and canyons over time
moving earth to create deltas and islands

Steady and clear in its fluidity
silky and caressing
gentle as the ocean on a quiet day
as it pushes into the sand
creating beaches
places of beauty to rest
and renew the spirit

Until a storm strews turmoil and
the galloping waves crash
raking the beach and reclaiming
the sand it has seeded

Water nourishes the earth in all its forms
pillar of life
bringing peace to the soul
Great is the strength of water
mighty in all its manifestations
yet soft and pliant to the touch

So is the strength of women
No need for armor or
the bastions of war and power
No need for the battles of rock against rock

In nurturance and love is the true power
a fluid understanding that the flow is all
In time all surrender
to join the water as it flows

God's Cathedral

God's cathedral calls for no walls
a dirt path pulses
with the life of the Mother
stones and rocks
call forth ancient wisdom

A cathedral of trees
alive and knowing
tall gnarled trunks
with glorious leaves
of all shapes, patterns and colors

When I close my eyes
and listen to the bubbling brook
I feel the grace of the Beloved
move through me
whispering in the stillness
Open your heart to my love and blessing

Feet planted in the earth
I look at the sun
peeking through the trees
and feel the music of the heavens
singing praises of the Beloved
the Creator of it all

I Run

I run through the field
through the rain
in the sun and the clouds
on the soft and pliant earth
in the sky

I run
I am swift
I am sure
I am rhythmic
I am drums and music
I am singing birds
and flowing wind

I run
with arms out flung
I am joy
I am full
I am overflowing
I am all that I can be
I am free

I run
I am me

Sounds

I love the sound of thunder
in the distance
coming closer
the rumbling voice of Spirit
ready to water the world

I love the sound of lightning
crackling with energy
alive and vibrant
clearing the air of debris
making way for the rise of life

I love the sound of rain
soft and gently mesmerizing
drawing me in to listen
to the quiet pattering
that cleanses the earth
as it feeds the flora

I love the rapid pelting of the drops
of a great outpouring
creating puddles and rivers and streams
rushing water
a great cacophony of sound
clearing away dross
and opening the earth
to new growth

I listen
I love
I am in awe
I am at peace

Over the Fence

Over the fence I peek
trees dancing with the wind
in joyous reunion
caressing each other
A gentle waltz
whipping into a passionate tango
a playful foxtrot
gusts creating a quick step
raging into a paso doble

Wind and trees
against the skyscape of
cumulus clouds and baby blue
a bird gliding in the wind

Earth and heaven watch
in mutual enjoyment
as I do
as over the fence I peek

Sailing Home

Let's sail beloved says the Traveler
and marvel at the wonders
of the many worlds
Keep your eyes on the heavens
always tracking the direction home

So we sail
tacking left
tacking right
sailing through space time and dimension
all routes leading to the Beloved

We travel the infinite mysteries
we learn from the masters
and fly through the universes
through oceans and channels of
light and sound

We laugh as we glide through the stars
following the siren song of the angels
leading us home

Death

Death
an inevitability
sometimes sneaks up
like a monster in the dark from behind
as I scream from the shock
surprised and afraid
of a too soon ending of my life

Death
with her sickle
mowing down willy nilly
all who inadvertently
stand in her way

Death
no respecter of age
takes all whose time has come
ready or not
like the childhood game of hide and seek

Death
by bullet or bomb
sickness or starvation
accident or intention
the illness of old age
Grabs us all in a sudden burst
or long goodbye

Death
an angel of the afterlife
shepherds us to the next steps
on our journey
releasing the soul
from the illusions of the world

Death awaits us
harsh or gentle though the end may be
impartial witness
great equalizer
and guides us to the awakening beyond

In the Garden of Grace

I sit in the garden of your grace
breathing in the fragrance of the land

A multitude of flowers, trees, grass
each distinct
smells mingling
as I breathe in your presence

I sit in the garden of your grace
my vision filled with the beauty of your creation

A batch of yellow wildflowers
roses - red, pink, white, lavender
a rainbow of color drawing me in

Orchids with their infinite variety of
colors and shapes
blues, purples, golds dazzle me

Trees with sturdy and willowing trunks
with varying shades of green leaves
changing as the light meets them

I sit in the garden of your grace
feet bare feeling the texture of the earth
the tickle of the grass
the roughness of a nearby stone
the vibration of life in the bark of a tree

I sit in the garden of your grace
blessed in my meditation
at peace in the world

Marveling at the beauty and abundance
present in each breath

Inspiration

I wait
in pregnant pauses
waiting for the words to form
to give birth to a new phrase
a new thought

I wait
knowing I can't speed
the moment of birth
the burst of inspiration

The words stream out of their own accord
Forming sentences, phrases, verses
in poetic torrent
not written by me
but some unseen Spirit

I know now what the Greeks mean
when they speak of the Muses
the voices of Spirit
that give birth to the wisdom of the universe
and the beauty of the mundane

Art, music, poetry, dance
pour forth to teach and nourish
only after periods of gestation
in the hands of the masters
that sustain us all

Lattices of Light

Imagine a universe made of lattices
moving through space and time
all connected to the source

Webs of light and love
a great weaving
transversing worlds and dimensions
the very essence of creation

Silvery threads surround the earth
reinforced by the Light workers
strands stretching down into the planet
deep below into the center

Lattices and matrixes
at one with the cosmos
earth vibrating with
the energy of the One

Imagine these lattices
live deep within you
each organ, each cell, each atom, each quark
filled with lattices

Pulsating in rhythm to the whole
part of the great cosmic symphony
played by the Beloved

Imagine riding these lattices
as you step through time
exploring universes

Dimensions without end
time now, time then, time to be
all one in the now

Imagine strings of lattices
moving from your heart
to the heart of another
friend or imagined foe

Woven into the oneness
each person, each creature connected
each strand filled with the essence of love

Knowing this how can we hold onto
our false sense of otherness
we are all part of this cosmic whole

I choose to focus on the love

Light

The Divine presence awaits and awakens within

I Stand As A Battery

I stand sometimes as a cross
arms wide
feet planted on the earth
crown open
Light flowing through me

Like a battery connected to
the heavens and the earth
positive and negative polarities
work together to channel the Light

The flow continues gathering power
fueling the infinite connection
to the source of all things
while grounded to hold the energy here

Living fully between the worlds
the Light through me is anchored to the planet
and the earth's fertile energy fills the heavens
with its endless possibilities

I stand sometimes as a cross
magnetized and alive
vibrating with the glory of the earth's cradle
and the heavens that fill me to the core

I stand as a battery
open to the call of Spirit
as the Light channels through me
nourishing and alive in its splendor

Blank Canvas

Today
A blank canvas waiting to be filled
in a moment of inspiration
or in a random impulse
to lead me one way or another
to my first brushstroke of the day

Which color will I use
which shape
as I face the unknown
I wait for the day's direction to emerge
to follow the path laid out
by the spirit within

With faith I approach the canvas
peaceful in the knowing
that whatever strokes I take
if I fill them with love
the day will be filled with Light
no matter the shadows that might emerge

I Hold A Candle

I hold a candle
it flickers in the dark
caught for a moment in the breeze

I hold a candle
renewed and burning bright
shining light into the darkness

I hold a candle
a point of light
attracting others

I see flashes in the distance
flickering in and out
Another candle and another
forming circles around the shadowed center

Surrounding the darkness with light
illuminating the way
the darkness retreats
in the face of an ever-growing array of lights
until it is but a shadow in the corner

So light your candle
and hold it
Join the bearers of Light
as we open the doors to a new world

I hold a candle
flaming bright
as may we all
harbingers of a world to come
messengers of the Light

Painted Sky

I look above and see the sky
a painting in the air

It seems to be a master's work
of clouds with feathered streaks
with brushstrokes through of baby blue
striations in the sky

With mountain peaks and pillow tops
that funnel far away
it looks as if the waves have moved above
a pattern in the high

To see the breadth and capture it
is a daunting task
if I could paint
I think I could get closer to the truth
I'd add the depth and endless pulse
that brings it all to life

Yet though I'd strive
I'd miss it still
no matter how I tried
for who am I with earthly hands
to capture the Divine

God's canvas touched with
Her great Light
it is an awesome sight
the master of earth's beauty paints
and fills the soul with light

Anchored

Have you noticed
how some anchors
allow for a pliability
vessel moored
yet moving and bobbing
drifting ever so slightly in the water

So am I
anchored to the Light
I move and bob
through the adventure of life
falling overboard at times
to be caught and dried off
on Mother's soft earth

Yet drift though I may
I am tethered with good solid
ropes of Light
keeping me moored
to the Beloved
in all that I do

Reaching for the Light

Tree branches twist to find the sun
to feed on the light that sustains them
dwarfed in the darkness of the forest

Plants unbalanced in the effort to reach the sun
leaves grow lushly basking in the light
stunted in the shadow

So am I reaching for you Beloved
for the warmth of your Light
for the healing of your love

Yearning for your Light to shower me
in the warmth of your being
and chase away the shadows of separation

I turn to you Beloved
craving your touch
so I may grow and flourish
in this world of shadow and light

The Light That You Are

I shed my garments Beloved
to stand naked before you
Will you clothe me in your glory?
Embrace me in your love?
As I surrender all to the ineffable presence
that surrounds me ever more

I surrender
I have said I surrender,
and said it again and again
in my wish to make it so
Yet as a tease does
I have held back a piece of myself
afraid of completing my union with you

I tire of the repetition of separation
weary of the effort it takes to maintain
that piece of aloofness
to keep my mind from disintegrating
into the chaos it fears

Ready to let go at last
I dissolve in the wonder
of the nothingness and everything
of your being
in the place beyond words
I breathe in the Light that You are

God is Here

God is here
in each breath God lives
God is in the eyes of the lover and stranger

God is here
I call and Spirit fills me
I turn away and am left alone

God is the compass
that guides me on my journey home

God is infinite
beyond words and understanding
writing about God is a ghost of Her essence

As I journey and search
I lose my way as I forget
that wherever I am on my path
God is

Ever present
waiting for me
to turn into
Her embrace

Innocence

Shall I fall back into your arms Beloved
surrendering to your ineffable presence
trusting that you will catch me
to hold me in your gentle embrace

Will you raise me ever higher
as I laugh in exaltation
in my journey with you
through the worlds without end

All sins of my imagination shed as we travel
I shine in the Light of your connection
naked in my innocence
I see the purity of the soul that I am

I welcome the great adventure of being
knowing you are there to hold me
and I am forever connected to my source

Bathing in the Light

I bathe in the light of the Beloved
rays of multicolors streaming through me
from the heavens
grounding in the earth

I bathe myself
twirling in the sun of your Being
as I am immersed
in the crystalline beams of your light

I bathe in your plenty
in your infinite love
your grace and acceptance

I bathe in the joy of your Being
in the Light of your presence

I bathe myself and give thanks

Peace

Peace
Stillness
The nothingness of empty thoughts
Forever silent
except for the wind
the dogs
the rustling leaves

Peace
A quiet heart
The solid core
Like the trees
growing deep
rooting in the earth
branching in the sky

Clear and unafraid in the knowing
that when all the trappings of the world drop away
this remains
the earth
the sky
the peace and beauty of the soul

Peace
In certainty that here and now
I sit in the perfection of God's glory
in the stillness of all being
with the lattices that connect us
to the infinite source

This peace and loving
is ever present
when I stop and listen
and look around
breathing deep the essence of the Spirit
that is in all things

I Am An Instrument

I am an instrument
to be played
to be tuned
to be practiced on

At first a bit discordant
with practice, over time
I open to the music of Spirit
A melodious sound comes forth

Cleaned and polished till I shine
my strings are plucked and bowed
a melody takes form
I play and am played
opening ever more to the sound

I follow the call
of the music of the Divine
transcribing and writing
the music pours through me
I know my purpose

I am an instrument of Spirit
bringing forth the Light and
sounds of the Divine

Compassion

As I walk through the fields of suffering
I open my heart

Holding
as the grief of the world flows through

I join with the compassion of the Beloved
and the pain is transmuted
in the ever present Spirit

Emerging as a river of love and Light
to fill the world

Rock Me In Your Arms

I am weary my Beloved
Hold me in your arms
lift me above the tensions
and the stresses of the world

Raise me to the heavens
that I may bathe in your Light
refreshed for the next round of battle

Help me to give up the battle
that I might win the war
Opening my heart
to love with the very core of my being

Lift me to the stars
rock me in the cradle of the heavens
to rest in the oneness of all being

Fly me in your arms
so I might see the rhythm of all things
and move beyond the limits of my vision
and my mind

Enter through my crown
opening my third eye
Fill me with the glory of your Being
as I remember again my source

My soul yearns for the unity
that my mind disdains and turns from

Guide me through my well-built walls
the obstacles I've placed along the way
Cut through my armor
To unfurl in the sunlight of your splendor
translucent with your Light

Hold me in your arms
help me to know your love
and my own

I marvel at the peace and joy
of being with You
as I rest on my journey home

The Nexus

At the nexus of destruction and creation
lies the Light
shining through the pinpoint of the now
magnifying like a telescope
the vastness of the universes

Be still and focus

It is here that we stand and enter into the unknown
it is the entrance to the mystery schools
and beyond
the point of total silence
and a constant humming of God's name

Feel the vibration in this moment
sense the universe contained within
This place that has no words
connects all to the source
and to each other

It is here that we stand
holding the light of healing and love
Each consciousness connected
in the web of light crisscrossing the earth
through the servants of the Light

At this nexus of creation and destruction
the Divine presence awaits
and awakens within

The Weaver

Woven lattices of light
look and you can find them in all things
thin threads connecting all to the Beloved

Spiraling threads boring through
time and matter
filaments of light connecting all in a oneness
that eludes those who would
separate and deny
those who would emphasize our differences

As if we could be different
all woven from the same matter
connected by filaments and lattices of light

Look at the beauty in all things
see the glory of God in each other
and in all creation
for all has been created by the One
the Weaver of the lattices of light

The Lighthouse Keeper

In the darkness
lost
without direction

A faded light pierces the fog
reflected in the dim mirror
of the ocean's turbulent water
showing a direction to those lost
and floundering at sea
a route to follow to safe harbor

Is it a true light or a mirage
creating hope in the blackness that surrounds?

Drawn I follow the light
hoping it is real
and not the jagged pieces of my fractured mind
trying to make sense of it all
in the channel of illusion I have been navigating

I follow and as I do
the light brightens the sky
glowing and shimmering with the
endless array of colors making up
the whitest of light

Entranced by the radiance engulfing me
I follow without thought
the twinkling light to its source

I see ahead a lighthouse
beaming light in all directions
inviting me to land and
immerse myself in the warmth
and grace of Spirit's call

I view through my bedazzled eyes
a figure approaching
the lighthouse keeper
who weaves a tale of the power of the Light
sent forth to comfort all
in the darkest of nights and times

The lighthouse keeper
brings hope, peace and love
to a world torn asunder by the dark forces
within and without

Breaking the illusion of the darkness
with the Light
Piercing the deepest fog with
the greatest power of all
the gift of Spirit

Throughout the world the beacons shine
inviting all to come and
join in the amplification of the Light
of the source connecting us all

Bathe in the purity of this Light
Shower in the multifaceted colors of the universe
Fill to overflowing with the bounty of the Light

Join the lighthouse keepers
Beam the light of the divine flowing through you
as it radiates in all directions

Be a beacon in the dark
standing with the keepers of the Light
engulfing the darkness in iridescent perfection

Ever connected to the truth of who you are
at one with the Light

Acknowledgments

Thank you to all who have helped me in the creation of this book. To Andrea my love and my editor. This book would not be in its current form without her. Thank you to my spiritual teachers, the Travelers, who guide me on my path. They teach me the power of love, inner spiritual awareness, and to look for the Divine in all things.

Thank you to Lisabeth Reynolds, poet and friend, for the many hours spent sharing poems and ideas. Her editorial assistance was invaluable. Thank you to Susan Tabin who read this book and gave me valuable feedback.

Thank you to Donna Hollinshead for supporting me and my poetry. Without our spiritual work together this book would not exist.

I am ever grateful to all my friends who listened to my poetry along the way and encouraged me to share it with the world.

My heart sings in gratitude for the loving and grace of the Beloved who resides in my heart, guiding me as I navigate this world of shadow and Light.

Biography

Jacqueline Miller lives in Florida with her wife and two cats. She loves nature, walks, dancing, and photography. Her forty years of spiritual study inform her world view and inspire her poetry. Connecting to Spirit fills her with joy.

Jacqueline has worked as a psychotherapist, educator, spiritual counselor, and clinical social worker assisting people of all ages on their journeys of self discovery. She now provides spiritual counseling through private sessions.

She has been writing poetry for much of her life. This is her first collection, with more to come.

Made in the USA
Las Vegas, NV
01 December 2024